George Washington's Invisible Enemy

by Marie Richter

HOUGHTON MIFFLIN HARCOURT
School Publishers

PHOTOGRAPHY CREDITS: **Cover** © The Granger Collection, New York. **Title page** Archives Charmet/The Bridgeman Art Library. **3** © The Granger Collection, New York. **4** © North Wind Picture Archives. **8** Private Collection/The Bridgeman Art Library. **12** © Getty Images. **14** © Francis G. Mayer/CORBIS. **15** © The Granger Collection, New York. **16** Archives Charmet/The Bridgeman Art Library. **17** © CORBIS.

Printed in China

ISBN-13: 978-0-547-01666-5
ISBN-10: 0-547-01666-2

13 14 15 16 0940 19 18 17 16
4500569761

Table of Contents

Introduction

The enemy was silent, stealthy, and undeniably deadly. It attacked day and night, summer and winter, north and south. It afflicted man and woman, soldier and civilian, young and old. Wherever a group of people congregated, the enemy flourished. In its wake, it left open sores, fever, nausea, internal bleeding, anxiety, and death. It was called *smallpox.*

The year was 1777. The American Revolution had been raging for two years. General George Washington, commander of the Continental Army, had settled in with his troops to wait out the winter at Valley Forge, Pennsylvania. He was preparing to fight two foes—the British forces and the deadly smallpox virus.

Fighting against the British troops would not resume until spring, but fighting smallpox was a continuous task. Washington was desperately in need of an effective strategy to use against smallpox.

The winter was harsh at Valley Forge, Pennsylvania, in 1777.

The Smallpox Epidemic: A Hidden Enemy

Smallpox is a disease that killed approximately 60 million people worldwide during the 1700s. It killed so many because it is an infection that is easily passed from person to person by physical contact or inhalation of germs.

Smallpox begins with flu-like symptoms—fever, nausea, headache, and backache. Intense anxiety can also occur at this stage. Next, blisters form inside the mouth and nose as well as on the face, arms, neck, back, and feet. Eventually, a victim may die, either from massive internal bleeding or from other complications. In the 1700s, one out of three people who caught the disease died. Those who survived had to deal with lifelong scars, deformities, or even blindness.

Colonial America was in the midst of a smallpox epidemic when the Revolutionary War began. In Europe, smallpox was a common problem. People tended to catch the disease when they were young and had a better chance of survival. Many British soldiers fighting in America had survived smallpox and were thus immune to the disease.

Immunity occurs when the body becomes resistant to a disease. Anyone who caught smallpox once could never catch it again. The Continental soldiers, however, were not so fortunate. In fact, during the first two years of the war, hundreds of men who joined the army to fight the British died of smallpox. Thousands more refused to sign up, for fear of the legendary disease.

George Washington knew that because of the smallpox epidemic, he had a serious problem on his hands. This dilemma was not the first one he had faced in his life.

Fortunately, earlier experiences had taught Washington to be a creative and effective problem-solver. Washington's father died when George was just 11 years old, and he spent his early adolescence living with his mother. He received a grade-school education at home. Then he began a career in the military.

Much of his more advanced learning took place on the battlefield. He was 21 years old in 1753, at the start of the conflict that became the French and Indian War. As Major Washington, he was in charge of leading expeditions into enemy territory. He made mistakes. He lost soldiers. Through it all, he survived the crises. He earned a reputation as a leader who exhibited courage even when faced with almost impossible odds.

Ambitious, capable, and incredibly self-disciplined, Washington became a man who preferred giving orders to taking them. He did not fear going against public expectations. This trait would prove particularly important in dealing with the smallpox epidemic.

Young George Washington made decisions based on instinct and experience.

Washington was a man of action. He could not sit idly by to watch disease ravage his Continental Army. It was difficult enough fighting a war with poorly trained troops, a lack of supplies, and a disorganized Congress. In addition to those difficulties, up to one-fourth of his regiments might be sick with smallpox at any one time.

Washington himself was immune to the disease because he had contracted it on a trip to Barbados in 1751. For nearly a month, he had battled the illness. As a survivor, he understood both the horrors and the dangers of the disease. And as a leader, he devised a plan to deal with the epidemic during the war.

First, he quarantined any soldiers who already had the illness. This meant that he kept them apart from other soldiers until they were completely cured. Second, he decided that all new recruits should be inoculated against smallpox.

To inoculate a person, a small dose of the smallpox virus was introduced through a scratch on the person's skin. The immune system could fight the smallpox virus on the skin more easily than if the person had contracted smallpox through airborne germs. That meant the chances of recovery were much greater. After recovering from the small skin infection, the person would be immune to smallpox thereafter. This process is also called *immunization.*

Making sure that all his soldiers received immunization was not a simple task for Washington. In today's world, children grow up receiving immunizations within the first days and months of their lives. Medical advancements have eliminated or greatly reduced the spread of diseases such as smallpox, chickenpox, mumps, and measles.

The very idea of giving germs to someone to prevent disease was virtually unheard of in colonial America. The idea was so new and so untested that many colonists were afraid to try it. Their fears were not unfounded.

Inoculation's Early Days

Imagine that someone offers you a treatment that could prevent you from getting one of the deadliest diseases in the world. There are only two downsides to the procedure. First, you might get sick or even die from the treatment. Second, you would be contagious for about four weeks. This means that you could possibly spread the disease to others. Would the risks be worth the benefits? For many colonists considering smallpox inoculation, the answer was *no*. Fortunately, several visionary leaders, including George Washington, answered *yes*.

Inoculation, Immunization, and Vaccination

These terms describe the same basic procedure—***making a person resistant to a disease by exposing the immune system to a mild or related version of the disease***. The immune system quickly develops a way to fight off the mild virus or bacteria. If the person encounters the disease again, the immune system will fight it. The inoculated person will not get sick.

Lady Mary Wortley Montagu was a writer and explorer. She introduced inoculation to Europe.

The idea of trying to prevent disease through intentional exposure has its roots in Asia many hundreds of years ago. It wasn't until the early 1700s, however, that Europeans began experimenting with various methods.

Lady Mary Wortley Montagu was an Englishwoman married to the British ambassador to Turkey. In 1715, when she was 26, she contracted smallpox. Although she was scarred by the disease, she survived.

Living in Turkey, Lady Montagu saw many people who had also suffered from smallpox. She also saw an unusual treatment to prevent its spread. In Turkey, people took scabs from smallpox pustules and ground them into a powder. Then they dipped a needle into the powder and plunged it into the arm of an uninfected person.

Another variation of the treatment involved dipping needles in the pus that gushed from open sores. The needles were then used to insert the pus into a healthy person's vein. The concept became known as *inoculation.* It was a method of infecting a person with a weakened strain of a disease to prevent a more dangerous form from developing.

Lady Montagu praised Turkish inoculation methods when she returned to England. Because of her influence, doctors and patients soon began to develop their own experimental versions of the process.

Lady Montagu had introduced the life-saving practice of inoculation to Europe. However, her ideas did not enjoy the same sort of public attention or approval across the Atlantic Ocean. Ideas traveled slowly. Bringing inoculation procedures to the colonies created controversy.

Public opinion in the colonies was opposed to the procedure. People thought it was too risky. When a minister named Cotton Mather encouraged widespread inoculation in Boston in 1721, people were so outraged by the idea that they attacked his house.

Even 50 years after Lady Montagu brought inoculation to Europe, Continental Army leaders were extremely afraid of spreading smallpox. In fact, Continental soldiers were forbidden to receive inoculations. In 1776, General Benedict Arnold issued a formal decree that promised "severest penalty" for any army surgeon who performed inoculations. Officers caught getting inoculated would be dismissed. Army privates would be punished by court martial.

The threat of discipline did not discourage everyone. Some soldiers were so desperate to escape the disease that they secretly tried to inoculate themselves. They tried to do so by scraping contaminated pins underneath their fingernails.

George Washington's Decision

Thus, George Washington's plan to inoculate the troops at Valley Forge challenged popular beliefs. Washington was far less concerned with public opinion than he was with preserving the lives of his soldiers and the strength of his army.

Washington recognized that inoculation came with dangers and responsibilities. Nonetheless, he made the decision that he felt was in the best interest of his soldiers and his country. Not every decision a leader makes will be a popular one. Sometimes controversial orders must be given. As Washington saw it, the alternatives to inoculation—dying soldiers, British domination of the battlefield, and retreat and even the possibility of surrender—were unthinkable.

General Washington also had evidence to suggest that the British were *intentionally* trying to contaminate Continental troops with smallpox. According to an American sailor, British general William Howe sent smallpox-infected people to the outskirts of Boston in 1775. His alleged goal was to infect Continental soldiers. Washington suspected that smallpox was "a weapon of Defence [our enemies] Are useing against us," as he wrote in a letter to Congress.

Historians have never been able to prove for certain that the British were trying to use smallpox as a weapon. Still, the fact that Washington suspected such a problem gave him even more reason to inoculate his soldiers.

Inoculation at Valley Forge

George Washington's plan was simple and effective. Camped at Valley Forge during the winter of 1777, troops who had never caught smallpox would be inoculated. Then they would be quarantined for the several weeks it took them to recover from the disease and get over being contagious. Inoculated soldiers were placed in a large barn. The barn was separate from the rest of the camp. The inoculated soldiers would have no contact with other men until their allotted time was up.

While this plan worked to make many soldiers immune to smallpox, it presented its own danger. If the British had found out that large numbers of Continental troops were quarantined and unable to fight for weeks at a time, they might have attacked Valley Forge and overpowered the weakened American men. Inoculation, then, had to happen secretly and swiftly.

If you were a soldier arriving in Valley Forge to join Washington's army, your first order would have been to undergo smallpox inoculation. First, you would be given a scratch on the arm. The scratch would then be covered with a fresh smallpox scab. Over the next few weeks, you would be quarantined. During that time, you would develop what was hopefully a mild case of the illness.

The Continental Army built cabins at Valley Forge.

If you got quite sick, you would be placed in a hospital cabin. Not everyone in the hospital cabin would be suffering from smallpox. Some patients might have other complaints such as dysentery, boils, or frostbite.

Chances are, you and your fellow patients would not have enough blankets to keep you warm. Freezing currents of winter air would blast through gaps in the walls. The cabin would often be bitterly cold. With luck, you might have a bed to lie on. Unfortunately, you would probably have to share it with bedbugs and lice. A mixture of sulphur and tallow (animal fat used to make candles and soap) might be spread on your itching sores. Still, there was no anesthetic for numbing the pain.

Being a soldier in the Continental Army was not an easy task. Even if you did not fall ill, you had to endure bitterly cold conditions with very little food and supplies. The winter at Valley Forge was brutally hard on Washington's soldiers, but it was a strategic step toward winning the war.

How Inoculation Helped Win the War

Washington's troops emerged from their winter at Valley Forge poorly dressed, underfed, and lacking in military supplies. But they were immune to smallpox. This important fact changed the course of the war in several ways.

First, men who were previously hesitant to join the army for fear of infection now could join without fear. The number of recruits and re-enlistments at Valley Forge swelled over the winter of 1777–1778. By the time spring arrived, Washington's army had grown considerably. Historians believe that between eight and twelve thousand men were gathered at Valley Forge, prepared to fight on behalf of the newborn nation. They marched out of their camp in May 1778 and entered a new phase of the war. Now victory was not just a dream shimmering on the horizon; it was a very real possibility.

Second, with his troops inoculated, Washington could send soldiers into regions where smallpox was rampant without worrying about losing men to the disease or further spreading the disease. In Charleston, South Carolina, for example, soldiers assisting the Continental Army refused to enter the town because smallpox was on the loose. Washington sent his own inoculated troops in to retake the city. It was a magnificent victory against the British, and one that eventually helped secure the South.

General Washington reviewed his troops.

Third, soldiers immune to smallpox foiled any possible plot by the British to use smallpox as a weapon against the Continental Army. Even if the British did try to contaminate Continental troops by exposing them to sickness, smallpox would have no harmful effect on Washington's soldiers. Washington could send soldiers wherever he needed them to go.

In part because of the smallpox inoculation, the Continental Army was well prepared to win the Revolutionary War. Some historians argue that Washington's approach to dealing with smallpox was the most important strategic decision he made during the course of his military career.

Smallpox: The Larger Picture

A disease like smallpox does not differentiate based on race, gender, social class, or nationality. While Washington's decision to inoculate his troops was a success story for the Continental Army, many other people living in North America in the 1700s suffered tremendously from the disease.

Because the disease had not previously existed on the North American continent, Native Americans had no immunity at all. Smallpox cases were very severe. Native Americans died in huge numbers. Some Native American populations were nearly or completely destroyed by smallpox.

By the late 1700s, smallpox inoculation had become more accepted. However, the opportunity to receive inoculation was also influenced by social class. For many colonists, it was too expensive a procedure. Often, the wealthy would get inoculated but neglect to quarantine themselves after the inoculation.

This caused people who had not been inoculated—often people who could not afford the inoculation—to catch severe cases of smallpox. Those at the bottom of the social ladder were left out of inoculation efforts. Thousands died in epidemics.

Many Native Americans died from smallpox.

Fortunately, over time, inoculation became a procedure available to all people. In 1796, an English doctor, Edward Jenner, introduced the idea of *vaccination* by using cowpox bacteria as a substitute for smallpox in the inoculation process. Cowpox resulted in a much milder reaction in patients, while still immunizing them to smallpox for the rest of their lives.

With the elimination of the risk of sickness from inoculation, the use of smallpox vaccinations spread worldwide, and the number of smallpox cases dropped dramatically. In time, as the result of so many people having been made immune to the disease, smallpox died out. The last known naturally occurring outbreak took place in 1977 in Somalia, Africa.

The term *vaccination* comes from the Latin root *vaca*, which means "cow." Edward Jenner performed the first vaccinations using the cowpox virus.

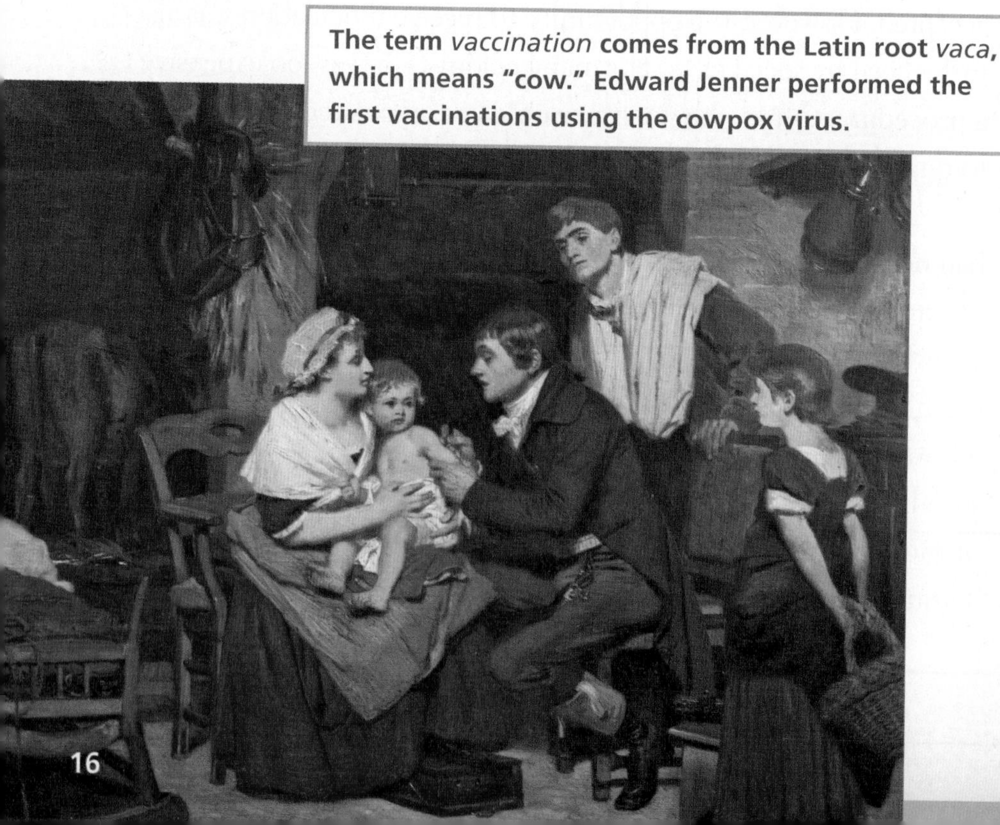

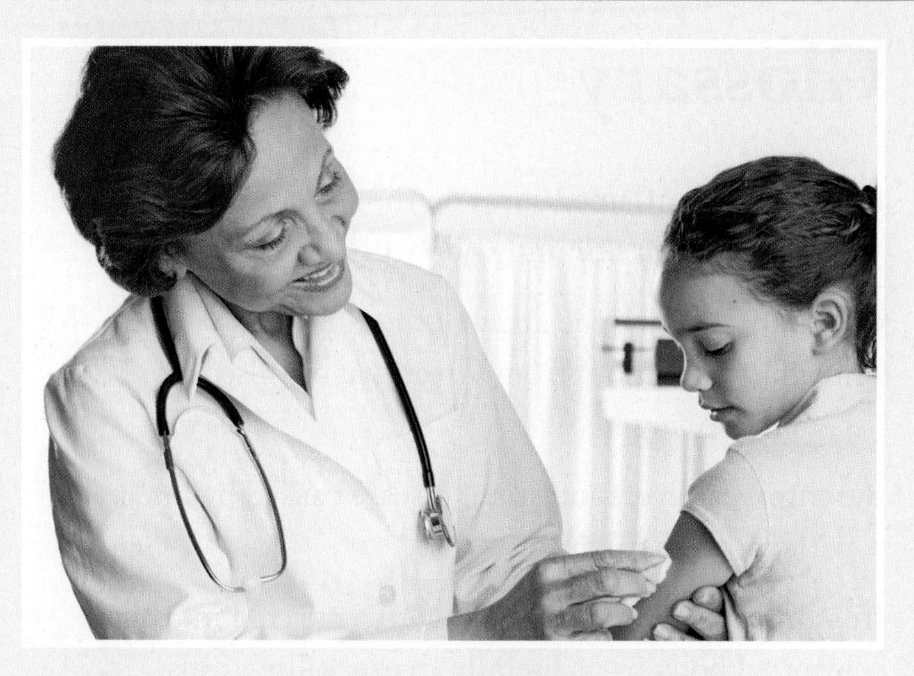

Smallpox in the Modern World

To this day, the smallpox virus still exists on the planet. Scientists keep several hundred vials in closely guarded laboratories for the purpose of studying the virus's structure. The disease, which caused so much pain and suffering in the past, may be able to provide us with discoveries that can improve human health in years to come.

Perhaps George Washington, a leader who tackled problems with courage and common sense, would approve of the current research. And if he had been able to see the future, no doubt he would have been delighted to know that the smallpox enemy he sought to contain has at last surrendered its force to strong leadership and the power of modern medicine.

Glossary

boils painful inflamed sores on the surface of the body, caused by deep skin infection with bacteria

Continental Army the army of the American colonies that fought for freedom from Great Britain; also called the Colonial Army

dysentery a severe intestinal disease caused by infection with bacteria or parasites

frostbite a condition caused by extreme cold in which external body parts literally freeze, killing cells

quarantine a period of time during which a patient must not have contact with anyone who can become infected with the patient's illness

Responding

TARGET SKILL **Conclusions and Generalizations** George Washington was not afraid to take risks. What details in *George Washington's Invisible Enemy* would lead readers to draw this conclusion? Copy and complete the chart below.

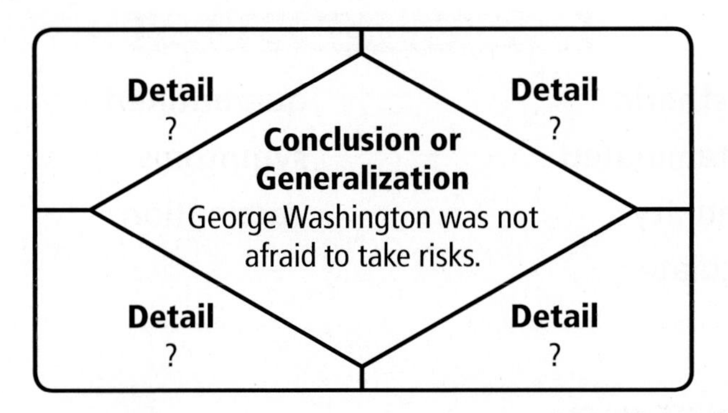

Write About It

Text to Text Washington's soldiers followed specific steps to avoid smallpox. Think of another story in which the characters follow a set of steps to accomplish a goal. Write several paragraphs explaining those steps.

TARGET VOCABULARY

foes	**plunged**
formal	**retreat**
gushed	**revolution**
legendary	**shimmering**
magnificent	**strategy**

EXPAND YOUR VOCABULARY

anesthetic	**quarantined**
contaminated	**symptoms**
immunity	**vaccination**
inoculate	

TARGET SKILL **Conclusions and Generalizations** Use details to explain ideas that aren't stated or are generally true.

TARGET STRATEGY **Analyze/Evaluate** Think carefully about the text and form an opinion about it.

GENRE **Narrative Nonfiction** gives factual information by telling a true story.